WORKING IN SPACE

Patricia Whitehouse

Heinemann Library
Chicago, Illinois

Designed by Heinemann Library
Printed in China by South China Printing.

08 07 06 05 04
10 9 8 7 6 5 4 3 2 1

Library of Congress Cataloging-in-Publication Data

Whitehouse, Patricia, 1958-
  Working in space / Patricia Whitehouse.
     v. cm. -- (Space explorer)
  Includes bibliographical references and index.
  Contents: Leaving Earth -- Jobs in space -- Astronaut training
-- Experimenting on astronauts -- Fixing satellites -- Working
outside -- Suiting up -- Gloves and tethers -- Moving around --
Working on other worlds -- Amazing space facts.
  ISBN 1-4034-5158-3 (library binding-hardcover) -- ISBN 1-
4034-5662-3 (pbk.)
  1. Astronautics--Vocational guidance--Juvenile literature. 2.
Space sciences--Vocational guidance--Juvenile literature. 3.
Outer space--Experiments--Juvenile literature. [1. Astronauts. 2.
Space shuttles. 3. Space stations. 4.. Occupations.] I. Title.
II. Series.
TL850.W49 2003
629.45'0023--dc22
                                                2003026769

Acknowledgments

The author and publishers are grateful to the following for
permission to reproduce copyright material:

Cover photograph: NASA

p. 4 NASA; p. 5 NASA; p. 6 NASA; p. 7 Science Photo Library;
p. 8 NASA; p. 9 NASA; p. 10 NASA; p. 11 NASA;
p. 12 NASA; p. 13 Science Photo Library; p. 14 Science Photo
Library; p. 15 NASA; p. 16 Science Photo Library;
p. 17 NASA; p. 18 NASA; p. 19 NASA; p. 20 Photri/ Topham; p.
21 NASA; p. 22 NASA; p. 23 Science Photo Library; p. 24
NASA; p. 25 Science Photo Library;
p. 26 NASA; p. 27 Photodisc/Getty Images; p. 28 NASA;
p. 29 (NASA/Science Photo Library

Every effort has been made to contact copyright holders of any
material reproduced in this book. Any omissions will be
rectified in subsequent printings if notice is given to the
publisher.

Special thanks to Geza Gyuk of the Adler Planetarium for his
comments in preparation of this book.

Some words are shown in bold, **like this.** You can find out
what they mean by looking in the glossary.

Contents

Leaving Earth

Five, four, three, two, one . . . The space shuttle blasts off! **Astronauts** on the shuttle are going to work. Some stay on the shuttle and some work at the **space station.**

Two astronauts have already started working. The shuttle commander is in charge of the shuttle and crew. The pilot flies the shuttle.

Three mission specialists are on board the shuttle. They work on **experiments** or climb outside to fix **satellites.** They have to prepare the food, too.

This mission specialist is measuring how far away the Hubble Space Telescope is from their space shuttle.

A company or university might want to do an experiment in space. An astronaut called a **payload specialist** will work on the experiment.

The payload specialist may have trained for two years just for this mission.

The space shuttle travels around Earth so fast that it is like falling. Everything inside falls, too. It makes **astronauts** and everything in the shuttle float around. This is called weightlessness.

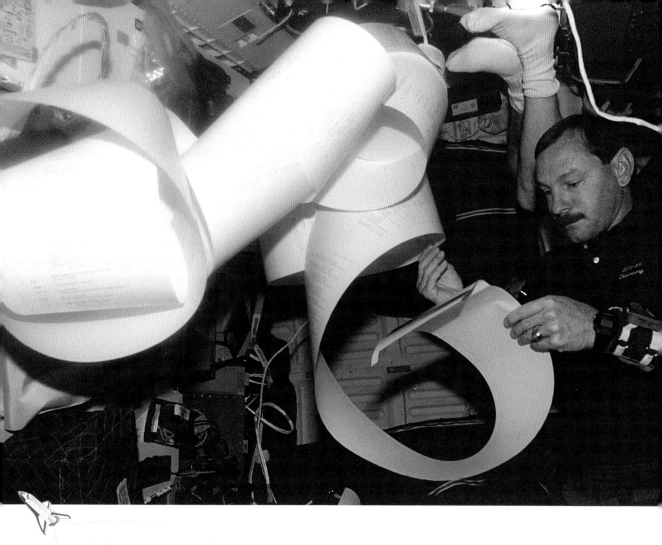

A long sheet of fax paper floats
in weightlessness.

Astronauts do not work at desks and
tables. Everything would float off because
of weightlessness! They have to use tape
to stick everything down.

Astronauts need special training. They study at a university and then do a year of basic astronaut training. Astronauts learn math, science, and **astronomy.** They also practice using space equipment.

Some equipment shows astronauts what it will be like to work in the International Space Station

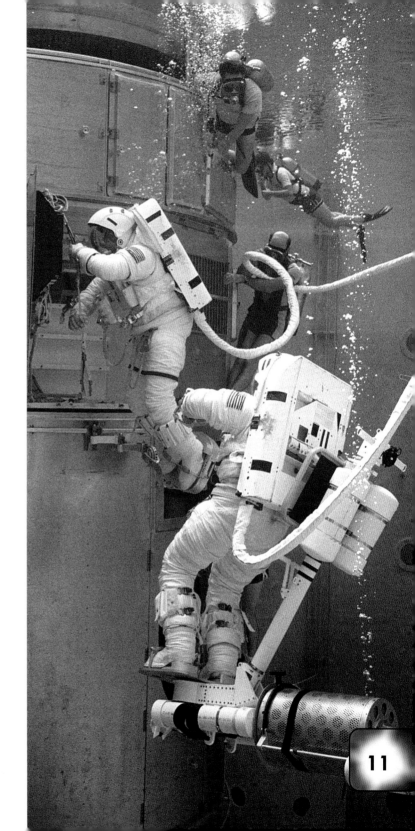

Astronauts practice working in water. Their suits are filled with air to make them float. It helps them learn what it will be like in space.

Under water it feels like you weigh less than on land. This is what it is like in space.

Experiments on Astronauts

Living in space can change the human body. **Astronauts** often take part in **experiments** to find out how to keep healthy in space.

This experiment measures how much air an astronaut uses while exercising.

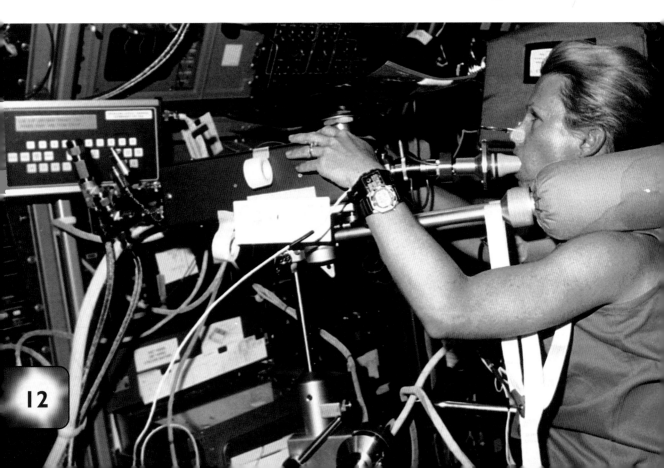

In space, astronauts do not use their bones and muscles very much. They can get very weak. Astronauts need to exercise every day in space.

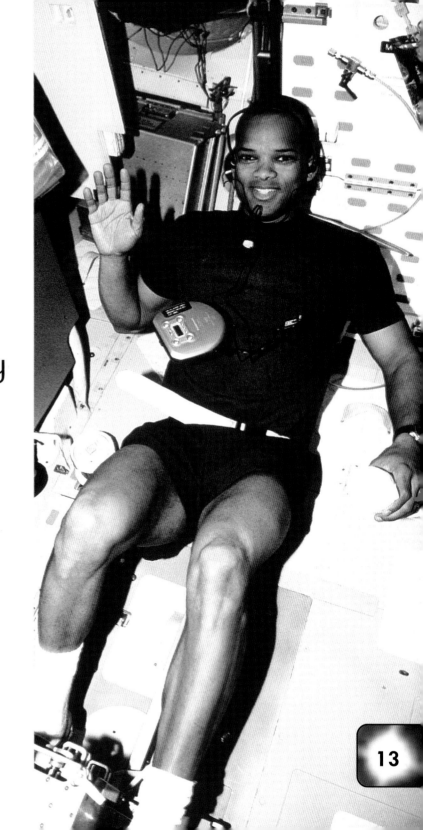

Scientists want to find out how living in space affects plants and animals. Astronauts have taken bees, ants, and fish into space to see what happens to them.

This experiment looked at how bean plants grow in space.

Astronauts also test to see what happens to chemicals in space. They use a sealed box with gloves sticking into it so the experiment does not float away.

Astronauts put their hands in the gloves so they can move objects around in the box.

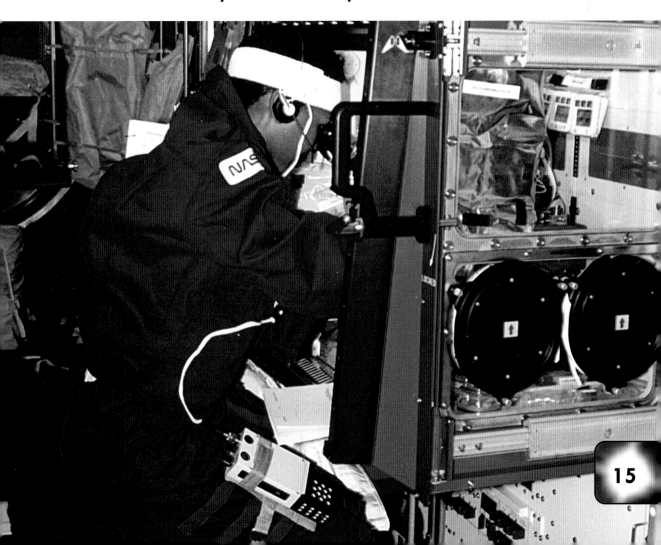

Astronauts also take pictures and videos of themselves living in space. The photos help people on Earth understand what it is like to live in space.

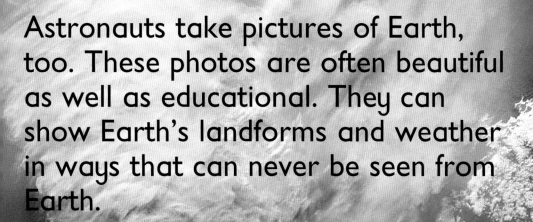

Astronauts take pictures of Earth, too. These photos are often beautiful as well as educational. They can show Earth's landforms and weather in ways that can never be seen from Earth.

Astronauts in space took this picture of a volcano erupting.

17

Satellites that **orbit** Earth sometimes break down and need repair. They cannot be taken to a workshop. Specially trained **astronauts** have to fix them.

The shuttle pilot finds the satellite and moves the shuttle near it. An astronaut uses the shuttle's **robotic arm** to pull the satellite into the shuttle's cargo bay.

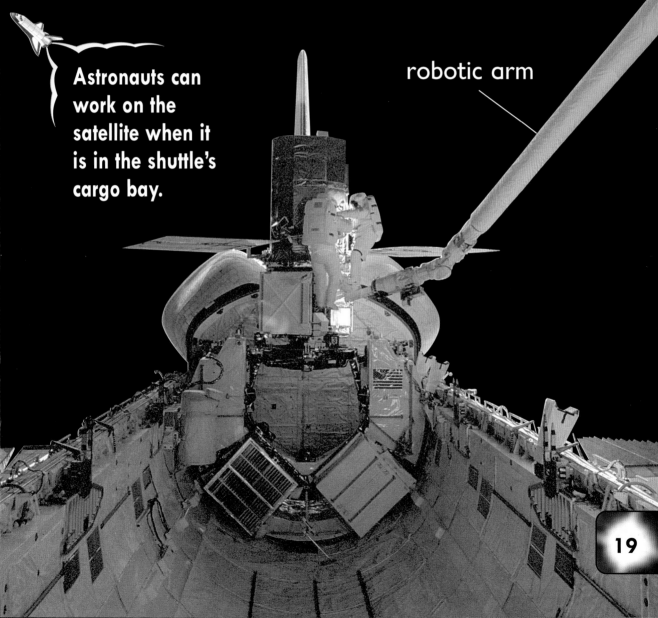

Astronauts can work on the satellite when it is in the shuttle's cargo bay.

robotic arm

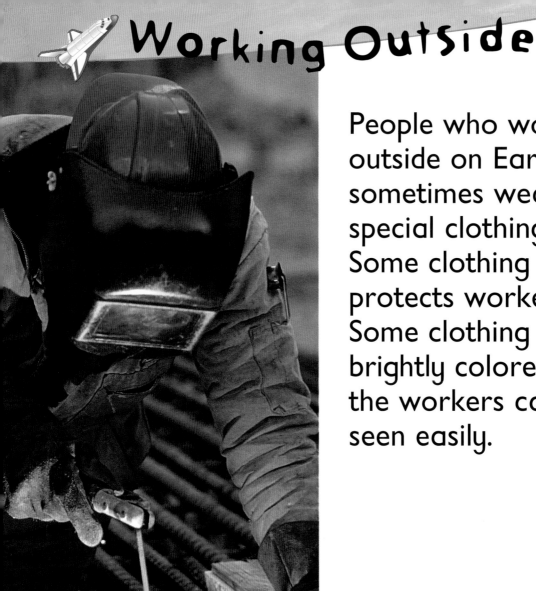

People who work outside on Earth sometimes wear special clothing. Some clothing protects workers. Some clothing is brightly colored so the workers can be seen easily.

A worker wears these clothes for protection.

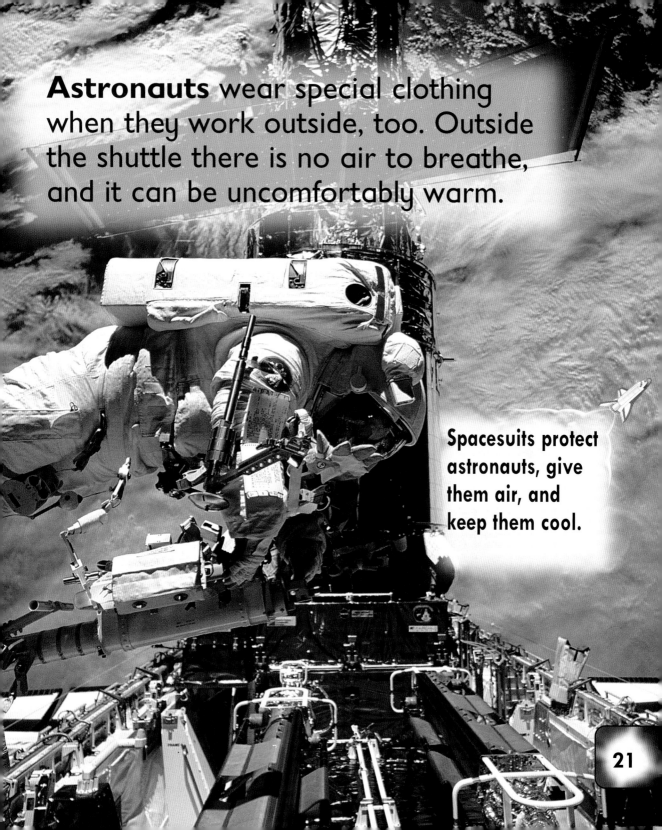

Astronauts wear special clothing when they work outside, too. Outside the shuttle there is no air to breathe, and it can be uncomfortably warm.

Spacesuits protect astronauts, give them air, and keep them cool.

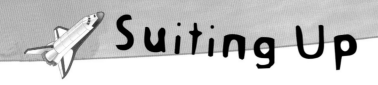

Suiting Up

Astronauts must wear special spacesuits to go out of the shuttle. The spacesuits allow the astronauts to breathe and stay cool. Every part of their bodies is covered.

Spacesuits are sealed at the neck, wrists, and waist.

Astronauts use an **airlock** to leave the shuttle. The airlock is a room between the shuttle and space. In the airlock, the door to the shuttle seals shut, and then the outer door into space can be opened.

Using an airlock keeps air from the shuttle from leaking into space.

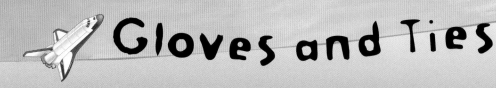

Gloves and Ties

Spacesuits are hard to move in. Gloves make finger movements tricky. Jobs that take a few minutes on Earth can take hours in space.

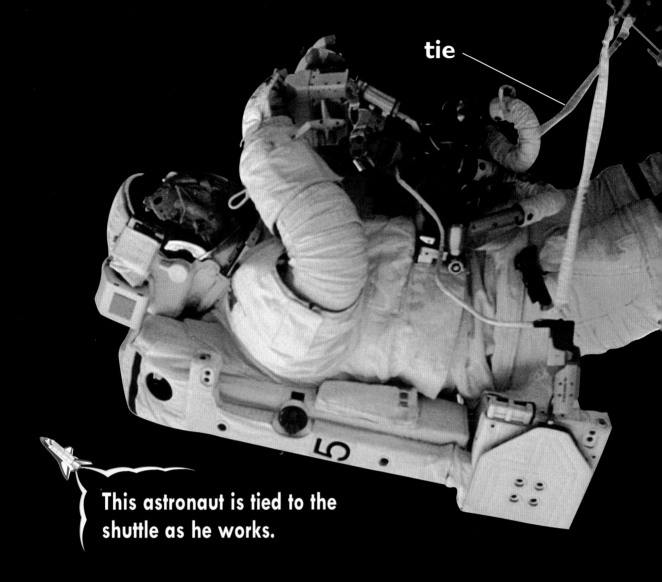

tie

This astronaut is tied to the shuttle as he works.

In space, **astronauts** and equipment can float away. Astronauts tie equipment to their suits. Sometimes astronauts are tied to the shuttle, too.

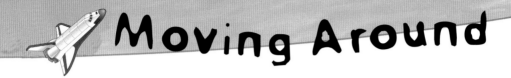

Moving Around

Sometimes **astronauts** need to move around a lot outside the shuttle. They wear a backpack with rocket power called a **Manned Maneuvering Unit,** or **MMU.**

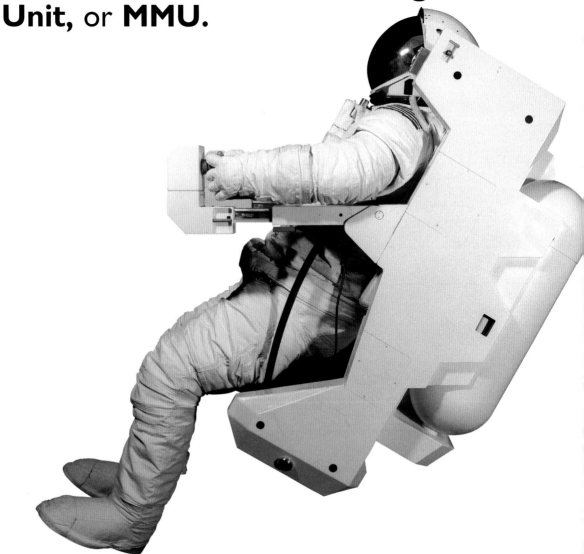

The MMU tank is filled with gas. The astronaut squeezes a handle, and gas comes out with enough force to move the astronaut around.

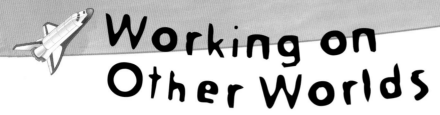

Working on Other Worlds

Twelve **astronauts** have worked on the Moon. They collected rocks from the Moon's surface. This helped scientists learn about Earth and about living on other worlds.

Scientists controlled where Sojourner went on Mars, and Sojourner sent photos back to Earth.

Scientists explored Mars using a remote-controlled robot called Sojourner. Scientists think that in the future people might be able to live and work on Mars.

Amazing Space Facts

- The longest time an **astronaut** has spent outside in a spacesuit is 8 hours and 56 minutes.

- It takes about 45 minutes for an astronaut to put on a spacesuit. Astronauts must help each other to put a spacesuit on.

- The largest-sized spacesuit weighs 107 pounds (48.6 kilograms).

- In the United States, more than 4,000 people apply for 10 astronaut jobs each year.

Glossary

airlock space between two doors that keeps air from escaping

astronauts people who go into space

experiments tests

Manned Maneuvering Unit (MMU) backpack with rocket power

orbit path one object takes around another

payload specialist astronaut working on university or company experiments

robotic arm remote controlled machine that can grab or move things

satellite object that travels around a planet or a moon

space station place where astronauts work and live in space

More Books to Read

Platt, Richard, and Leo Hartas. *Space Explorer Atlas*, New York: Dorling Kindersley Publishing, 1999.

Whitehouse, Patricia. *Living in Space (Space Explorer)*. Chicago: Heinemann Library, 2004.

Whitehouse, Patricia. *Space Travel (Space Explorer)*. Chicago: Heinemann Library, 2004.

Index